Teens
and
DISTRACTED DRIVING

By Jennifer Simms

ReferencePoint Press®

San Diego, CA

TEEN
Health
and
Safety

© 2019 ReferencePoint Press, Inc.
Printed in the United States

For more information, contact:
ReferencePoint Press, Inc.
PO Box 27779
San Diego, CA 92198
www.ReferencePointPress.com

Content Consultant: Despina Stavrinos, Assistant Professor, Department of Psychology, University of Alabama at Birmingham

LIBRARY OF CONGRESS CATALOGING-IN-PUBLICATION DATA

Name: Simms, Jennifer, 1978– author.
Title: Teens and Distracting Driving / by Jennifer Simms.
Description: San Diego, CA : ReferencePoint Press, Inc., [2019] | Series:
    Teen Health and Safety | Includes bibliographical references and index.
Identifiers: LCCN 2018011549 (print) | LCCN 2018012678 (ebook) | ISBN
    9781682825082 (ebook) | ISBN 9781682825075 (hardback)
Subjects: LCSH: Teenage automobile drivers—Juvenile literature. | Distracted
    driving—Juvenile literature.
Classification: LCC HE5620.J8 (ebook) | LCC HE5620.J8 S56 2019 (print) | DDC
    363.12/51—dc23
LC record available at https://lccn.loc.gov/2018011549

CONTENTS

Introduction   4

   A NAPKIN CAN TURN A FATHER
   INTO AN ACTIVIST

Chapter 1   10

   WHAT IS DISTRACTED DRIVING?

Chapter 2   24

   THE CAUSES OF DISTRACTED DRIVING

Chapter 3   38

   COSTS AND RISKS OF DISTRACTED DRIVING

Chapter 4   52

   HOW DRIVERS CAN PROTECT
   THEMSELVES AND GET HELP

   Recognizing Signs of Trouble/Organizations to Contact   68
   Source Notes   70
   For Further Research   74
   Index   76
   Image Credits   79
   About the Author   80

Introduction

A NAPKIN CAN TURN A FATHER INTO AN ACTIVIST

On their own, a taco, a box, and a text message are harmless. But put them in the hands of a driver, and the few seconds needed to take a bite, reach for an object, or type a reply can take a driver's attention off the road long enough to cause a crash.

Sometimes the consequences of the crash are minor. This was the case in 2017, when a semitruck driver in Washington State lost control and rolled his vehicle while eating a taco. No one was injured in the crash, but the road was closed temporarily as workers cleaned up the load of woodchips spilled over the two-lane highway.

Consequences were also minor for NFL player Nate Burleson when he crashed his hybrid in 2013. Burleson slammed his car into a concrete median when he reached for a pizza box about to slide off the passenger seat. He broke his arm in the crash, which shortened his season. He later posted photos with the caption, "I walked away from a totaled vehicle #blessed."[1]

> **"If you get a text, don't look at it. It's not worth it."[2]**
>
> —Liz Marks, car accident survivor

Other times, however, the consequences of distracted

4

driving are life-changing. Liz Marks was seventeen in 2012 when she glanced down from the road to read a text from her mother. Moments later, she rear-ended a tow truck stopped to make a left turn. Marks was airlifted to the hospital where she was treated for multiple injuries, most noticeably the loss of sight in her left eye. Marks now speaks out about the dangers of distracted driving. "If you get a text, don't look at it," Marks says in a National Highway Transportation Safety Administration (NHTSA) video. "It's not worth it."[2]

For Vijay Dixit, the distraction that changed his life was a napkin. In November 2007, Dixit's nineteen-year-old daughter Shreya was set to arrive home in Eden Prairie, Minnesota, to celebrate the Hindu festival Diwali with her parents and older sister. Shreya was a sophomore at the University of Wisconsin, Madison, and she had found a ride with a classmate who was also making the four-and-a-half hour drive that weekend.

About forty-five minutes out of Madison, the driver of the car Shreya was riding in swerved suddenly. The driver later told Dixit she was reaching for a napkin. As the car veered into the median, the driver overcompensated, ran through a culvert, and slammed the passenger side of the car into a concrete pylon. Shreya was airlifted to the hospital where she died a short time later. She was the only person killed in the crash.

As a result of that napkin and the choice of a young driver, Dixit and his wife Rekha were thrust into a world of unexpected grief. But with the help of a trusted counselor, they each found a way to live again. For Dixit, this meant starting the Shreya R. Dixit Memorial Foundation and campaigning to end distracted driving. As he explains in his book *One Split Second*, his work has helped him find purpose and helped him heal: "After losing Shreya we joined hands with new friends, local and national leaders, and great individuals who work

Distracted driving can cause car accidents. It is incredibly dangerous.

tirelessly on safety and driving issues, and none of that would have happened if Shreya had not been lost."[3]

Since 2009, the Shreya R. Dixit Foundation has hosted the Raksha Walk in Eden Prairie, a walk/5K run which raises community awareness about the dangers of distracted driving. Thanks to a petition by Dixit, Minnesota governor Mark Dayton declared the day of the walk Distraction-Free-Driving Day each year. In addition, the foundation awards stipends for drivers toward the cost of driver's education programs, conducts an outreach internship program for students, and sponsors Distraction-Free Driving clubs at local high schools. Dixit also speaks at local American Automobile Association (AAA) meetings, high schools, and businesses, sharing the story of his daughter and urging listeners to drive safely out of respect for fellow travelers on the road.

In 2017, the Shreya R. Dixit Foundation received the Star Award for Education at the Toward Zero Death Conference in Saint Paul, Minnesota, as a result of its work to end distraction-free driving. This award is given annually to Minnesotans who are leaders in the effort to improve traffic safety.

Through the years that have passed since the crash, Dixit and his wife have learned to live with the paradox of joy and sorrow that come from their situation. Dixit said, "We find joy in helping others share their stories of loss and finding healing, but at the bottom of it, we are doing this because we lost our child."[4]

Despite the efforts of safe-driving advocates like Dixit, distracted driving continues to be a problem throughout the United States. "It has been nine years since we lost Shreya," Dixit said in a 2016 interview, "but close to 3,000 more traffic fatalities have occurred in the nine years in Minnesota alone. In 2015, more than 400 died in traffic crashes. That number is unacceptable. Unless the trend is reversed, I will continue to say 'not much has changed.'"[5]

> **"We find joy in helping others share their stories of loss and finding healing, but at the bottom of it, we are doing this because we lost our child."[4]**
>
> —Vijay Dixit, author of *One Split Second: The Distracted Driving Epidemic: How It Kills and How We Can Fix It*

The number of people who die in car accidents each year is on the rise. Distracted driving may be one of the reasons.

When Dixit started his campaign in 2009, the total number of traffic fatalities in the United States was in a steady decline. In fact, it reached an all-time low in 2011. Since then, however, crashes and fatalities have been on the rise, with an 8.4 percent increase in 2015 and 5.6 percent in 2016. In fact, the 2015 increase was the biggest spike in fifty years.

"Insurance companies, which closely track auto accidents, are convinced that the increasing use of electronic devices while driving is the biggest cause of the rise in road fatalities," stated Neal E. Boudette in a 2016 *New York Times* article.[6] When phone calls and text messages were the main problem, accidents from distracted driving were decreasing. But Boudette believes that smartphone apps in particular are to blame for the rise in distracted driving accidents. As a result of the increase in crashes, advocates like Dixit, along with lawmakers and researchers continue to work together to make America's roads safer by educating teens and adults about the dangers of distracted driving.

> **"Insurance companies, which closely track auto accidents, are convinced that the increasing use of electronic devices while driving is the biggest cause of the rise in road fatalities."[6]**
>
> –Neal E. Boudette,
> *New York Times*

Chapter 1

WHAT IS DISTRACTED DRIVING?

The NHTSA defines distracted driving as "a specific type of driver inattention. Distraction occurs when drivers divert their attention from the driving task to focus on some other activity."[7]

There are three types of driver distractions. The first is visual distraction, meaning the driver's eyes are not on the road, like when looking at a cell phone screen. The second is manual distraction, meaning the driver's hands are off the steering wheel, like when adjusting the radio. The third is cognitive distraction, meaning the driver's mind is not thinking about driving, like when mentally replaying an argument with a friend. Sometimes an activity causes more than one type of distraction at the same time, making it even more dangerous. For example, retrieving an item from behind the seat can cause a visual and manual distraction. Texting, on the other hand, causes all three.

Often the term *distracted driving* is synonymous with cell phone use. And cell phones do create a wide variety of distractions, such as calling and texting, using music and mapping apps, taking photos, and updating social media. The popularity of the *Pokémon Go* mobile game in 2016 even tempted drivers to play games while behind the wheel.

Drivers can be distracted in many ways. Some distractions include using a phone or eating.

But distracted driving is broader than just cell phone use. It includes any activity that takes the driver's focus from the road. These activities include eating a hamburger or drinking coffee, adjusting the radio or climate controls, talking to other passengers, putting on makeup or shaving, reading the newspaper, managing young children, or driving with a pet in the car. Distractions can come from outside the vehicle, such as when a driver looks at an accident as she passes. They also include mental distractions, such as daydreaming or worrying. Any of these activities can steal a driver's attention, making her less capable of responding to sudden changes and increasing the potential for a crash.

In addition to distracted driving, there are many other ways a driver can become impaired and can cause a crash. Drunk driving, drugged driving, and drowsy driving are also types of driver impairment. Though these activities may at times be paired with distracting activities, they are not considered distracted driving. They have their own categories on police accident reports, and they have separate legislation that governs these behaviors.

Though awareness around distracted driving has increased in recent years, it is not a new problem. A 1969 study found that a driver's ability to see the road and make good decisions was impaired when he or she was talking on the early versions of car phones. In 2001, New York became the first state to pass a hands-free law, making it illegal to drive while holding a cell phone. Drivers can still talk on the phone, but they must be using a headset, speakerphone feature, or microphone through the vehicle.

More recently, distracted driving officially entered the national consciousness when, in 2009, Webster's New World Dictionary named it the word of the year. "I think its rapid intrusion into our national vocabulary shows what an epidemic distracted driving has become," former transportation secretary Ray LaHood commented on his White House blog.[8]

Since then, state and local governments have passed more laws to ban texting and other distracting activities while driving. Cell phone service providers have launched distraction-free campaigns. And victims of distracted driving have continued to speak about the consequences. Yet, despite these efforts, crashes continue to make headlines. A crash in Texas in March 2017, in which a twenty-year-old driver slammed into a church bus and killed thirteen senior citizens, made the national news. The cause of the crash: texting.

DISTRACTED DRIVING OR CARELESS DRIVING?

The actual number of distracted driving crashes each year is likely greater than the number reported in national statistics. Why the difference? According to the 2015 AAA study of teen drivers, "Police records frequently fail to identify whether or not distraction was involved in the crash."

Reasons police may underreport distracted driving include reliance on driver confession, the use of different crash reporting forms in different jurisdictions, and the tendency to report the cause of a crash as failure to obey traffic rules when it is difficult to prove driver distraction. This is what happened in the case of Michelle Begley, a Colorado woman killed while making a left turn in 2015. Eyewitnesses claimed the driver of the pickup that struck Michelle's car appeared distracted: he was looking in his lap and did not swerve or brake before impact. When police examined his phone, they found evidence of texting, but not at the moment of the crash. Since the cause of the distraction could not be proven, the driver was charged with failure to obey traffic signals for running the red light.

L. J. Blincoe, T. R. Miller, E. Zaloshnja, B. A. Lawrence, "The Economic and Societal Impact of Motor Vehicle Crashes, 2010 (Revised)," *National Highway Traffic Safety Administration*, May 2015. www.nhtsa.gov.

More Common Than People Think

Driver distraction may be more common than people realize, especially when considering the widespread use of cell phones. According to a 2018 study by the Pew Research Center, 95 percent of Americans owned cell phones and 77 percent owned smartphones. A 2017 study done by the automotive advocacy group Zendrive says drivers are using them with alarming frequency. The study analyzed 3.1 million drivers over a three-month period and found that in 88 percent of these driving trips, the drivers were on their smartphones. The researchers behind the study noted, "When extrapolated for the entire U.S. driving population, the number goes up to roughly 600 million distracted trips a day."[9]

Zendrive also found average phone use was 3.5 minutes per hour of driving time. "This finding is frightening, especially when you consider that a two-second distraction is long enough to increase your likelihood of crashing by over 20 times."[10] Even though the Zendrive study focused only on smartphone use and did not include other forms of distraction, distracted driving is clearly widespread on US roads.

> "This finding is frightening, especially when you consider that a two-second distraction is long enough to increase your likelihood of crashing by over 20 times."[10]
>
> —Noah Budnick, Director of Public Policy and Government Affairs for Zendrive

Distracted Driving and Road Fatalities

Statistics from the NHTSA show Americans are not only driving distracted, they're causing crashes. In 2015, 14 percent of all motor vehicle crashes reported by police were caused by driver distraction. According to the NHTSA report, 3,477 deaths and 391,000 injuries in 2015 resulted from distracted driving. These statistics include injuries or deaths of drivers and their passengers, passengers in other vehicles, and nonoccupants, such as pedestrians and cyclists. To put these numbers in perspective, more people were killed in distracted driving crashes in 2015 than the 2,977 killed during the terrorist attacks of September 11, 2001.

Distracted driving, however, is only one piece of the total driving fatality picture. Of the traffic fatalities in 2016, 3,450 were distraction-related crashes. This total is more than the 803 that were the result of drowsy driving. But it is less than the 10,497 fatalities resulting from drunk driving, the 10,111 fatalities resulting from speeding, and the 10,428 fatalities resulting from not wearing seatbelts.

Another statistic which worries road safety advocates is that driving fatalities in all categories have increased since 2011. In 2016, 37,461 people were killed on America's roadways, up from 35,092 in 2015. These annual totals are similar to the size of the student body at a large university. Along with a surge in the use of electronics, such as smartphones, researchers credit this spike in fatalities to lower gas prices and an increased number of jobs. When prices are low and people have more money, they drive more, creating the opportunity for crashes.

A 2015 study of teen drivers by the AAA Foundation for Traffic Safety, however, found that distraction may play a higher role in crashes than estimated in national statistics. According to the study, slightly more than half of the crashes for teen drivers were the result of driver distraction. "Potentially distracting behaviors in general, and cell phone use in particular, were much more prevalent in the current study than in official statistics based on police reports," the report suggested.[11]

Many safe driving advocates, including Jennifer Smith of Stopdistractions.org, understand the challenges of collecting accurate crash statistics. "Honestly, I think the real number of fatalities due to cell phones is at least three times the federal figure," Smith said in an interview with *Insurance Journal*.[12] According to Smith, one reason most distracted driving crashes go unreported is because it's so difficult for law enforcement officials to catch drivers in the act. "We all know what's going on, but we don't have a breathalyzer for a phone," Smith said.[13]

In addition, distracted driving crashes may be underreported because the data used to create national statistics is not standardized. National statistics are compiled from police reports, and the way officers diagnose and report the cause of a crash differs across the country. In a study by the National Safety Council (NSC) only about half of fatal crashes known to involve cell phone use were recorded as distraction-caused crashes in NHTSA databases.

Distractions That Cause the Most Crashes

In the case of drunk driving, there is only one cause: intoxication. But when it comes to distracted driving there are many possible causes. As a result, it can be challenging to determine which distracting activities occur most often and which are most dangerous. The 2015 study of teen drivers by the AAA Foundation for Traffic Safety tried to quantify which distractions are most likely to cause a crash.

In the study, teens ages sixteen to nineteen enrolled in a driver's safety course drove a car outfitted with a DriveCam system. These systems have sensors and forward and rear-facing cameras which record the eight seconds before and four seconds after a crash. Researchers analyzed the video of 2,229 crashes, examining the driver's behavior during the six seconds leading up to the crash and categorizing the types of distractions present.

According to the study, the top three crash-causing distractions were interacting with passengers (14.6 percent), cell phone use (11.9 percent), and looking at something inside the vehicle (10.7 percent). Additional distractions included looking at something outside the vehicle (9 percent), singing or dancing to music (8 percent), grooming (6 percent), and reaching for an object (6 percent). Researchers noted that teens in the study knew they were being filmed, so they may have been less likely to exhibit risky behaviors than the general teen population. As a result, researchers theorized

AMERICA'S DRIVE-AND-DINE CULTURE

Millions of Americans eat while driving. Though distracted driving is often synonymous with cell phone use, eating while driving is also a dangerous distraction.

McKeel Hagerty of Hagerty Classic Insurance examined his company's insurance claims and found the problem wasn't the food itself, but the mess. "It really seems it's more the spill than the eating," Hagerty said in an interview.[1] According to Hagerty, the ten messiest foods to consume while driving are coffee, hot soup, tacos, chili, hamburgers, barbeque, fried chicken, jelly or cream-filled donuts, soft drinks, and chocolate.

Why do Americans drive and dine? "The popular theory is we're all time-starved; we just don't have enough time in the day," says professor Stephen Bailey of Tufts University.[2] He describes eating while driving as the ultimate in multitasking. In addition, restaurants like McDonald's feed this desire with drive-through windows, and car makers enable mobile dining with multiple cup holders for the driver and passengers.

1. Quoted in Insure.com, "Some Foods and Drinks Can Lead to Dangerous Distractions," *Insure.com*, September 16, 2009. Insure.com

2. Quoted in Lucia Huntington, "The Real Distraction at the Wheel," *The Boston Globe*, October 14, 2009. Boston.com

that distracting behaviors may be even more common than reported in the study.

Another potentially dangerous distraction not accounted for in the AAA study is being lost in thought or daydreaming. A review of police reports by Erie Insurance suggests that this general distraction causes 62 percent of fatal distraction-related accidents. Other studies found lower percentages. Since it only occurs in the mind of the driver, this cause of crashes is very difficult to study. Researchers are working on ways to measure and reduce what they call "mindwandering."[14]

Distracted Driving's Effect on Teens

Distracted driving is dangerous for any driver, but it is especially risky for teens. A study funded by the General Motors Foundation in 2014 found that traffic crashes were the number one killer of teens. In addition, young adult drivers age fifteen to twenty cause a higher proportion of crashes each year than older drivers. Though young adults account for 5 percent of the total drivers in the United States, they were in 9 percent of traffic fatalities and 12 percent of overall police-reported crashes. This age group also had the highest proportion of drivers who were distracted when they caused a fatal crash.

Along with the increased risk for themselves, teen drivers are a danger to others on the road. When a teen causes a crash, nearly two-thirds of people injured or killed are people other than the driver. These victims include the teen's passengers, people in other vehicles, pedestrians, and cyclists.

Three factors increase a teen driver's risk of a fatal crash. The first is distracted driving, which plays a role in six out of ten teen crashes. According to the 2015 AAA study, crashes where the vehicle left the road and rear-end collisions were most likely to be caused by distracted driving. Not wearing seatbelts is the second factor cited for increasing the risk of a fatal crash. In 2015, 60 percent of teens killed in a crash were not wearing a safety belt. Reasons for not buckling up included forgetting or deciding it wasn't necessary because they weren't going far. The third factor in teen crashes is speeding. Nearly 30 percent of fatal teen crashes involved speeding.

"Alarmingly, some of the drivers ages 19–24 believe that their dangerous driving behavior is acceptable," said Dr. David Yang, AAA Foundation for Traffic Safety executive director.[15] "It's critical that these drivers understand the potentially deadly consequences of engaging in these types of behaviors and that they change their behavior and attitudes in order to reverse the growing number of fatalities on US roads."[16]

A 2017 systematic review of research on teens and distracted driving by the University of Alabama gives clues as to why distracted driving increases the crash risk for teens. The research team found that phone conversations, which create a cognitive distraction, increased the likelihood that a teen would make driving mistakes such as take a wrong exit, miss turns, fail to check mirrors, pause excessively at stoplights, and drive through yellow traffic signals.

> "It's critical that these drivers understand the potentially deadly consequences of engaging in these types of behaviors and that they change their behavior and attitudes in order to reverse the growing number of fatalities on US roads."[16]
>
> —Dr. David Yang, Executive Director of AAA Foundation for Traffic Safety

In addition, the review found that visually distracting tasks, like texting or reading an email, resulted in more frequent lane departures for teens than older, experienced drivers. They also found that tasks like texting made the driver's speed more erratic, as drivers tended to slow down while engaged in the task, then speed up once they had finished.

Is Distracted Driving Illegal?

There is no national distracted driving law. Instead, the federal government leaves it to each state to pass its own regulations. Fifteen states; Washington, DC; Puerto Rico; Guam; and the US Virgin Islands prohibit handheld cell phone use. No state bans all cell use

Texting and driving can result in a driving ticket in 47 states. Most states increase the fine for subsequent distracted driving tickets.

for all drivers, but thirty-eight states and Washington, DC, ban all cell use for novice drivers, and twenty states prohibit all cell use by school bus drivers.

Texting while driving is illegal in forty-seven states and Washington, DC. Texting while driving laws can be particularly hard to enforce, because a driver must confess they were texting instead of entering an address in GPS, which is frequently permitted. Other forms of distraction, such as reading a newspaper or eating, are often not regulated.

Laws also differ on what type of offense distracted driving is and how to enforce it. In some states it is a primary offense. A primary offense means a police officer can give a ticket directly to a driver for texting or eating while driving. In other states it is a secondary offense. This means a ticket can only be issued if the driver performs an unsafe activity that warrants a ticket. In these states, a driver couldn't be ticketed for texting unless he or she was committing another infraction, like swerving or running a stop sign.

A state law called Graduated Driver's Licensing (GDL) places restrictions on novice drivers so they can drive safely and distraction-free. GDLs usually consist of three stages. In the first stage, young drivers pass a test to receive a permit and may drive with a supervising adult in the car. In the second stage, the young driver passes a driving test and may drive alone but with restrictions. In this stage, many states ban cell phone use and night driving and restrict the number and the age of passengers. In the third stage, the driver earns a full-privilege license. States began creating these policies in the 1990s, and all US states now have some form of GDL.

In addition to state laws, many companies have distracted driving policies for their employees, usually centered around cell phone use. President Barack Obama signed an executive order in 2009 which banned federal employees from texting while driving. The ban applied to 4.5 million federal employees, including those in the military.

Trucking company Cummins banned all cell phone use, going further than state laws by banning the use of hands-free devices as well. "Many people were surprised to learn that the risk between hands-free and handheld cell phones were essentially the same," company spokesman Clint Wiernimont said in an interview with the NSC.[17] "The issue wasn't the phone itself; rather, in the cognitive distraction created by having a conversation. Cummins is a very data-driven company; given the data, in this case, the choice to include hands-free in the ban was justified."[18]

Do Distracted Driving Laws Work?

Proponents of distracted driving laws believe they are necessary based on the success of previous safe-driving campaigns. State and national laws have helped decrease risky behaviors such as not wearing seat belts or drunk driving. Limited research has been conducted on the effectiveness of distracted driving laws, however, and the studies that have been done present mixed results.

A 2014 study from the University of Alabama at Birmingham found a positive correlation between distracted driving laws and a reduction in crashes. It found that laws banning teen drivers from texting were the most effective. Traffic deaths in this age group decreased 11 percent in states with these bans. They also found that state-wide handheld cell phone bans were most effective at reducing traffic deaths for drivers ages twenty-one to sixty-four. But laws were found to be ineffective in states with only secondary enforcement laws.

> **"Thus, even as states increasingly are enacting laws limiting drivers' phone use, it is unclear the laws will have the desired effect on crashes."[19]**
>
> —Insurance Institute for Highway Safety

However, a 2014 study by the Insurance Institute for Highway Safety reviewed crash report data in states with and without distracted driving laws and determined it to be inconclusive. "Thus, even as states increasingly are enacting laws limiting drivers' phone use, it is unclear the laws will have the desired effect on crashes," the study reported.[19]

A 2017 study by Zendrive also found laws and driver behavior don't always align. The study ranked states from least to most distracted by calculating "the ratio between the average daily trip time

22

and the average amount of time drivers used their phones each day."[20] When they compared this list to states with strict hands-free laws, the results were mixed. In theory, states with strict hands-free cell phone laws should top the list for the least amount of driver distraction. However, two of the ten most distracted states, Vermont and New Jersey, have hands-free laws, and several other states fell in the middle of the ranking. When analyzing cell phone use by city, Zendrive found that drivers in Los Angeles, in a state with a hands-free law, spent more time on their phones than in any other city.

There are several reasons distracted driving laws may not reduce cell phone use or the number of crashes. One reason is that the laws can be hard to enforce. Drivers may drop their phone when they see a police officer or try to conceal it in their laps. Another reason may be that the laws focus only on cell phones, while a variety of other distractions such as interacting with a GPS or just general mental distraction are not regulated. Another factor, according to a 2012 study from Massachusetts Institute of Technology is that drivers who drive with a cell phone tend to drive more aggressively in general. "It's great we can take the phone out of their hands, but these may be the drivers who are getting in accidents anyway," study leader Bryan Reimer explained in an interview with *Science* magazine.[21]

Though it may be unclear whether or not distracted driving laws are effective, it is clear that distracted driving is widespread among teens and adults in the United States and many lives have been changed or lost in distraction-related crashes. As a result, researchers are working hard to determine the causes of distracted driving, who is most likely to drive distracted, and what can be done to prevent it.

Chapter 2

THE CAUSES OF DISTRACTED DRIVING

Singing along with a song. Taking a selfie. Arguing with a passenger. There are numerous ways a driver can become distracted. And research shows teens are more likely than other age groups to cause a distracted driving crash. In fact, several factors make teens more susceptible to distractions and more likely to crash. In addition to their lack of experience behind the wheel, how teens use their cell phones, how their brains are developing, and the influences of their friends and families make teens more likely to drive distracted, putting themselves and others at risk.

Teens and Cell Phone Use

One risk factor that makes teens more likely to crash is cell phone use. Many safe-driving advocates see this as the most dangerous distraction for all drivers because it causes all three types of distraction: visual, manual, and cognitive. Texting is the most dangerous phone activity because all three types of distraction occur at the same time.

In addition, the number of teens with cell phones continues to rise, increasing the number of teens who may become distracted while driving. In 2017, eMarketer found that 88.3 percent of adolescents ages twelve to seventeen owned a cell phone and that 84 percent of those adolescents had smartphones. Based on data collected over several years, the group predicted the total number of teens with cell phones would increase to 92 percent in 2019.

Teens with cell phones spend a lot of time using technology each day. Common Sense Media surveyed teens with smartphones in 2015 and found they spent an average of four hours and thirty-eight minutes on their phones each day. The number one way teens use their phones is accessing social media services, followed closely by listening to music. Other activities include playing games, watching online videos, and video chatting. And teens are using their phones everywhere: at home, at school, and in the car.

In addition to social media and entertainment, teens use their phones to communicate with friends and family. About 90 percent of teens with cell phones text regularly, and the average teen sends and receives sixty texts per day. That number climbs to one hundred texts per day for teen girls ages fourteen to seventeen, the group that sends the most out of any demographic.

Research shows that teens don't put down their phones when they get behind the wheel. According to a 2015 survey by State Farm, 90 percent of teens say they know it's dangerous to text while driving, but 44 percent admit to doing it anyway. In addition, the survey found that teens admit to driving while doing other potentially distracting behaviors, including listening to a navigation system (79 percent), searching for music (73 percent), accessing the internet from their phones (36 percent), reading social media (29 percent), or taking pictures (27 percent).

Though people may be quick to blame teens and their phones for the rise in distracted driving, some studies have found adults are also to blame. A 2012 survey by AT&T found that adults are actually

CONFIRMING HANDS-FREE VERSUS HANDHELD DANGER

A 2014 NSC public opinion poll found 80 percent of drivers believe it is safer to use a hands-free device than a handheld phone while driving. State laws agree. Though 15 states ban handheld phone use, no state bans hands-free devices. However, more than thirty studies claim that hands-free is just as dangerous because it's the conversation, not the device, that distracts the driver. So who's right? In an August 2015 episode of Discovery Channel's *Mythbusters*, hosts Adam Savage and Jamie Hyneman decided to find out.

For the experiment, the show partnered with Stanford University to determine the difference in drivers' safety when using a handheld and hands-free device. Using Stanford's state-of-the-art driving simulator, they challenged thirty volunteer drivers to follow audible navigation directions and avoid obstacles while talking on the phone. Of the fifteen drivers using a handheld device, one passed the test. And of the fifteen drivers using a hands-free device, the same number—just one—passed. "Hands-free and hands-full drivers were equally dangerous," Savage said of the test results. "Well, there you have it," said Hyneman. "Don't use your cell phone while you're driving."

Quoted in "Hands Free vs Handheld Minimyth." *Discovery.com*, August 2015. www.discovery.com.

more likely to text while driving, with 49 percent of adults admitting to the behavior. The higher crash-rate for teens may be a result of inexperience, and not just increased cell phone use.

Cell Phone Addiction

If teens know that using a cell phone while driving is dangerous, why do they do it anyway? One possibility is that cell phones are addictive.

As a result, the physical and mental compulsion to continually check for texts or posts overrides the teen's knowledge of the risks. In fact, in another Common Sense Media survey, half of teens and just over a quarter of adults reported they felt addicted to their phones.

David Greenfield, founder of the Center for Internet and Technology Addiction, explained this addiction in a 2015 interview with the *Huffington Post*. According to Greenfield, users who compulsively check their phones are trying to stimulate their brain's reward system. "It's very neurologically addicting," Greenfield said.[22] "When you get a hit—finding something or hearing from someone, you get an elevation of dopamine, and it compels us to keep checking."[23] Thanks to dopamine, a hormone that creates the expectation of positive feelings, reading a text or getting a like on a photo creates a burst of pleasure. Greenfield compares this obsessive pleasure-seeking to a gambling addiction.

"Smartphones are essentially the world's smallest slot machine," Greenfield said.[24] "Every time you go on your phone, whether to look at a Facebook update or check your email, you never know what you're going to get and how good it's going to be."[25]

In addition, researchers have found that adolescents are more susceptible to addictive behaviors than other age groups because the reward system in their brain is still developing. Daniel Siegel, author of the 2014 book *The Power and Purpose of the Teenage Brain*, calls this "brain remodeling," and says it's necessary in preparing the teen to leave home and become an adult.[26] "Dopamine levels at baseline are lower, and the dopamine release amounts are higher [in adolescents]," Siegel says.[27] This difference compels teens to seek activities that boost pleasure. But if teens repeat these pleasure-seeking activities, such as excessive cell phone use, they can actually change the way their brain functions at the cellular level, rewiring it to crave the activity more and more.

Social media platforms like Snapchat want to keep users returning to their app. This adds to peer pressure to keep up with social media communication.

Cell phone addiction may not, however, be the fault of the user alone. Companies that make cell phones and apps design them to exploit the brain's reward system and keep their users hooked. Tristan Harris, a former Google product manager, spoke with CBS about how companies purposely use features such as notifications, likes, and followers to compel people to check their apps more frequently and stay on them longer. According to Harris, more time spent on an app means more advertising dollars and more in-app purchases for the company. As an example, Harris explained how Snapchat compels its users to access the app:

So Snapchat's the most popular messaging service for teenagers. And they invented this feature called "streaks," which shows the number of days in a row that you've sent a message back and forth with someone. So now you could say, "Well, what's the big deal here?" Well, the problem is that kids feel like, "Well, now I don't want to lose my streak." But it turns out that kids actually when they go on vacation are so stressed about their streak that they actually give their password to, like, five other kids to keep their streaks going on their behalf. And so you could ask when these features are being designed, are they designed to most help people live their lives? Or are they being designed because they're best at hooking people into using the product?[28]

In addition to cell phone addiction, teens and adults also feel pressure from friends and family to be available and respond promptly to calls and texts at all times. Seventy-two percent of teens and 48 percent of parents feel the need to immediately respond to texts, social-networking messages, and other notifications. For teens, the reasons to stay connected are mostly social, but for adults, work can add pressure as well. For example, adults can feel the need to respond promptly to customers so they don't miss making a big sale. As a result, it can be very difficult for teens and adults to put down the phone, even when getting behind the wheel.

Multitasking and Driving

Another reason teens and adults post to Facebook, eat a sandwich, or put on lipstick while driving is the belief that they can multitask safely. But research shows that even if the driver's eyes remain on the road, he or she cannot do two things at the same time and do them both well. A video produced by TEDPartners explains it this way: "Our brain is not wired to pay attention to more than one complex task at a time. What we're actually doing when we think we're multitasking is quickly shifting from one thing to another."[29]

At times, it may not feel like the brain is doing much while driving, especially on a long, empty stretch of road. But researchers argue that safe driving requires a high mental effort or cognitive workload. Even when traffic is light and road conditions are good, there are several activities a driver's brain should be doing at all times to operate the vehicle safely. Distracted driving researcher David Strayer created the acronym SPIDER to describe these activities.

First, the driver should scan (S) for visual threats. These threats could be other cars, pedestrians, or objects that may get in the way. Next, a driver must predict (P) where unseen threats may arise. For example, the driver should predict a car could run a red light at an upcoming intersection. Based on what they see and predict, a driver must then identify (I) actual threats, like an actual car speeding toward them and decide (D) when and how to act in order to safely avoid the threat. Finally, the driver must execute a response (ER), such as to brake, change lanes, or turn. These steps represent a continual process, as the driving environment constantly changes.

When drivers are multitasking while driving, their brains become overloaded and are not able to process all the information their eyes are seeing. Even when a driver has both hands on the wheel and her eyes are straight ahead, her brain can be distracted, missing important objects and events around her. This is what happened to a 20-year-old woman in Michigan in 2004 who was talking on her cell phone when she ran a red light. Witnesses to the crash said the woman was looking straight ahead as she passed four cars and a school bus stopped in the lane next to her. She struck a car crossing the intersection, killing a twelve-year-old boy. The fact that the driver missed several important cues (stopped cars, a red light, crossing traffic) and struck the car without applying the brakes showed that even though she was looking out her windshield, she was not comprehending or reacting to her environment.

Researchers call this phenomenon inattention blindness. This happens because the driver's attention is focused on the conversation and there are not enough brain resources left to process everything they see. Drivers engaged in a phone conversation can miss up to 50 percent of what's happening around them. As a result, drivers are four times more likely to crash while talking on the phone and eight times more likely to crash while texting.

Knowing the Risk and Driving Distracted

Another reason teens and adults continue to drive while distracted is something researchers call optimism bias. Optimism bias describes the tendency of the human brain to assume the best. When people hear that texting and driving can lead to a fatal crash, their optimism bias leads them to believe this may happen to someone else, but it won't happen to them. According to a University of Wisconsin study, optimism bias, or a sense of invincibility, is stronger in teens than adults. "Teens are especially likely to underestimate their susceptibility to harm or the severity of potential negative consequences of some behavior, and this belief increases the likelihood that they will engage in the behavior."[30]

People drive while distracted because they feel a false sense of confidence in their driving ability. Research shows drivers tend to believe their distracted behaviors are not as risky as they are for other people. A study by the NSC found that two-thirds of drivers felt unsafe because of other drivers' use of technology, but only a quarter of those surveyed felt their own technology use was dangerous.

"Teens are especially likely to underestimate their susceptibility to harm or the severity of potential negative consequences of some behavior."[30]

—University of Wisconsin study

Finally, there's a misconception among drivers that an action isn't dangerous because nothing bad has happened. Every time a driver talks on a cell phone or drinks coffee while driving and doesn't cause a crash, she will feel more confident that her distracting actions are actually safe. The reality is, the driver's behaviors aren't safe—instead, the driver is just fortunate. As Brian Fielkow, CEO of trucking company Jetco Delivery, tells his drivers, "You can get away with texting and driving or using a handheld several times, and that leads you to the false conclusion that it's safe. It's not. You're just lucky. And that day of reckoning is going to come."[31]

Teens, Adults, and Risk-Taking

One reason teen drivers are more likely to crash is that they are more likely than adults to take risks in general. Sarah-Jayne Blakemore, who studies adolescent brain development, put it this way: "Teens are headed toward adulthood and need to explore the world to find their own place and sense of security. And exploring means taking risks."[32]

In addition to their need to explore their world, teens are more likely to take risks than adults because the part of their brain that controls impulsive action isn't fully developed. In fact, it won't be fully developed until a person reaches his or her mid-twenties.

> **"Teens are headed toward adulthood and need to explore the world to find their own place and sense of security. And exploring means taking risks."[32]**
>
> —Sarah-Jayne Blakemore, Professor of Neuroscience at University College London

Another reason teens take risks is because they are more sensitive than adults to what their peers think of them. Just as the reward system of the brain lights up when a person checks his or her cell phone, the reward system also reacts when teens get positive feedback from their

Driving with a lot of peers increases the chance for distraction and a wreck for teens. Inexperienced drivers should only drive with an experienced driver in a passenger seat.

peers. If risky behavior gets positive attention, the teen will feel good and want to do it again.

This desire for peer approval explains why teens are more likely to engage in risky behavior while driving with other teens in the car. A study published in the *Journal of the American Medical Association* found that drivers carrying passengers were more likely to run a red light than those driving by themselves. In addition, a review of studies on young drivers by Marie Claude Ouimet found that having teen passengers increased the risk of a crash. She also found that teens were more likely to not wear their seatbelts, follow too close to the car ahead, and get distracted when driving with other teens.

As a result, a car full of teens is especially dangerous. The risk of a crash increases by nearly half when an inexperienced driver has one teen passenger, the risk doubles with two teen passengers, and it quadruples when there are three or more. And the risk is greater for a group of males. As Nichole Morris, a safe-driving advocate in Minnesota, explains, "The reason for that is you have this group think—'Isn't it fun if we all speed,' or 'Let's not wear our seatbelts, none of us!'"[33] Morris goes on to explain that the crash rates for female teen drivers also increases with additional female passengers, but the increase isn't as dramatic.

In addition, research shows personality plays a role in whether or not a teen will choose to drive distracted. A study by the University of Alabama surveyed teens ages sixteen to nineteen about their personalities and their driving behavior and found that certain types were more prone to distracted driving. Extroverted teens were most likely to text and use their cell phones while driving, which fit the researchers' hypothesis. Surprisingly, conscientious teens were almost as likely to engage in the same distracting behaviors. Researchers expected this group, known for being organized and dependable, to be more careful behind the wheel. Instead, they found these teens' desire to be responsive to friends was greater than the compulsion to follow safety rules. Teens who ranked high in agreeableness were the least likely to use phones while driving. "The cooperative nature, including respect for rules and authority figures . . . may make them less likely to engage in distracted driving behaviors," researcher Despina Stavrinos explained in a press release.[34]

Families and Distracted Teen Drivers

Several studies show that families play a significant role in whether or not a teen will drive while distracted. Teens will often imitate their parents, and many parents are setting a bad example. A 2012 study by Liberty Mutual Insurance and Students Against Destructive Decisions (SADD) found that teens who witness their parents unsafe driving behaviors are more likely to follow suit. Staggeringly, 91 percent of teens reported that their parents talk on cell phones while driving, and 90 percent admitted to the same behavior. As for texting, over half the teens said their parents had sent a text while drive and three-quarters said they'd done it as well.

Teens also report feeling unsafe with their parents' use of technology while they drive. "I am concerned because when my mom drives she talks on the phone a lot so she is still alert but she can get kind of dangerous," a middle-school aged boy said in a Pew Research Center survey.[35] In the same survey, a teen boy reported, "Yeah, my [dad] drives like he's drunk. His phone is just like sitting in front of his face, and he puts his knees on the bottom of the steering wheel and tries to text."[36]

> **"I am concerned because when my mom drives she talks on the phone a lot so she is still alert but she can get kind of dangerous."[35]**
>
> —Anonymous respondent to Pew Research Center survey

Additionally, families put pressure on adolescents to be available at all times, even while driving. A study by the NSC found that 82 percent of all drivers felt that family was the highest motivation to engage in distracting behaviors like talking on the phone or texting while driving. In a study funded by the National Institutes of Health (NIH), researcher Noelle LaVoie found that 50 percent of teens with an unrestricted license had talked on the phone with a parent while driving. "Teens said parents expect to be able to reach them, that parents get mad if they don't answer their phone and they have to tell parents where they are," she said.[37] The study also found that teens are more likely to text their

Pulling over to the side of the road to take a phone call is much safer than driving and talking. If the shoulder of the road is not safe, a parking lot can suffice.

friends than parents, but that family texts do contribute to the overall number of texts sent and received while driving.

According to LaVoie, the message is clear. "Parents need to understand that this is not safe and emphasize to their children that it's not normal or acceptable behavior."[38] She encourages parents to ask their teens, "'Are you driving?' If they are, to tell them to call you back or ask them to find a spot to pull over so they can talk."[39]

Distracted Driving Versus Drunk Driving

People often compare distracted driving to drunk driving because the consequences of both actions can be deadly. "Cell phone use while driving is the new drunk driving—drunk driving 2.0," Susan Yum wrote in an editorial for the *Huffington Post*.[40] Yum's five-year-old son was killed when their car was struck by a texting driver in 2011.

According to researcher David Strayer the comparison is valid. "Someone who is talking on a cell phone is about as likely to be involved in an accident as someone who is drunk," Strayer said in an online interview.[41] In a 2006 study, Strayer found both types of driving were equally dangerous but for different reasons. In a situation where the driver needed to stop, a distracted driver tended to brake too late or not at all, while a drunk driver tended to follow too closely and brake too hard. Another difference was that a drunk driver knew he or she was impaired and tended to overcompensate by driving slower or stopping earlier. In contrast, distracted drivers didn't realize they were impaired and didn't exhibit extra caution.

Harvard University researcher Jay A. Winstin agrees that most distracted drivers don't realize they're a danger on the roads. "There's absolutely no social stigma connected with distracted driving today—unlike drunk driving, which took years to develop," Winstin said in a 2017 interview with the *Chicago Tribune*.[42] Instead of being embarrassed about driving distracted, Winstin finds that most people are arrogant about their actions. "If someone asks me at a cocktail party what I'm working on, and I say distracted driving, they'll laugh and talk about their own behavior," he explained.[43]

Winstin, who worked to popularize the concept of a designated driver in the late 1980s and 1990s, believes this attitude toward distracted driving won't end until society views it with the same shame with which it views drunk driving. "We need to create that stigma. We need to create a sense of shame connected with the behavior of driving distracted, which doesn't exist today."[44]

Chapter 3

COSTS AND RISKS OF DISTRACTED DRIVING

Most of the time, when teens or adults drive while distracted, nothing tragic happens. This lack of immediate consequences can give drivers the false belief that they are superior multitaskers and that their distracted behavior is safe. But when these risky behaviors eventually catch up with them and the drivers do cause a crash, there are many consequences. These include financial costs, legal penalties, serious injuries, or even death.

Monetary Costs of Crashes

Distracted driving crashes have significant financial costs both to society and to the individual who caused the crash. In 2010, the NHTSA estimated that the total cost to society for distracted driver crashes in the United States that year was $39.7 billion. This amount represented 16 percent of the total cost for all motor vehicle crashes that year. When calculating this cost, the NHTSA considered a variety of factors. They included costs to the individual from not being able to work and having to pay medical expenses, costs to insurance companies, and costs to the community for things such as road closures and legal expenses.

In addition, the NHTSA calculated that each critically injured survivor costs society an average of $1 million. This calculation includes the cost of the person's ongoing medical care plus the loss of their ability to work and earn money. The cost for each fatality is an average of $1.4 million. More than 90 percent of this figure is the income this person would have generated over his or her lifetime and legal costs.

Effects on the Driver's Insurance

Another way to look at the financial cost of a distracted driving crash is to consider what a driver must pay as a result of causing the crash. Any driver who causes a crash can expect his or her auto insurance rates to increase, but when the driver is a teen, it can be especially costly. Just insuring a new teenage driver is expensive. "Teenage drivers are considered to be among the highest risks for auto insurance and pay correspondingly high premiums for their first few years of coverage," says AutoInsurance.org.[45] Parents adding a teen to their family policy can expect their monthly bill to increase anywhere from 50 to 100 percent. And in many states, teen boys are more expensive to insure than teen girls.

> "Teenage drivers are considered to be among the highest risks for auto insurance and pay correspondingly high premiums for their first few years of coverage."[45]
>
> —AutoInsurance.org

Each state has different laws governing auto insurance, and each insurance company has different policies regarding what happens after a crash. But teen drivers who cause a distracted driving crash could see their rates more than double. For example, a male teen in Pueblo, Colorado, would pay $1,101 every six months for auto insurance to a national insurance company. If that teen causes one accident, his insurance cost would increase to $2,637. In addition, parents' insurance rates can also increase if the teen is a secondary driver on their vehicles. Increased rates last for three to five years and then begin to drop if the driver doesn't file additional insurance claims.

In some states, an insurance company can cancel the teen's coverage or choose not to renew it if the teen is ticketed for a serious violation or if the costs of the crash are significant. If this happens, the teen will either need to stop driving, because most states require a licensed driver to have auto insurance, or enter the state's assigned risk insurance pool. This high-risk pool is funded by voluntary contributions from insurance companies. The uninsured driver can get coverage from the high-risk pool, which is typically more expensive, and will need to keep a clean driving record for several years to be a candidate for traditional insurance.

If a person is hit in a distracted driving crash, the insurance company of the person at fault in the crash will cover the victim's car repair costs and medical expenses. Depending on state laws, however, the crash victim may also see an increase in his monthly insurance rates, though the increase would not be as high as if he had caused the crash. Some states, like California and Oklahoma, prohibit insurance companies from raising rates for the person who is not at fault. In a collision where both drivers were at fault, both drivers' insurance companies will split the expense.

Consequences of a Ticket

Drivers face both financial and legal penalties for driving while distracted. In states where distracted driving is a primary offense, drivers can get a ticket even if they don't cause a crash. Police officers can give a driver a ticket just for texting or other distracted behaviors.

In states where texting and driving is a primary offense, it can result in a ticket. In states where it is a secondary offense, drivers can still receive a ticket if their phone use causes them to break another law.

In states where distracted driving is a secondary offense, he or she must break another traffic law before police can ticket the driver.

State laws also vary as to what types of distraction can merit a ticket. In some states, like Missouri, texting is banned for drivers twenty-one and younger but not for adults. In other states, like Oregon, any hands-on cell phone use is considered a primary offense for teens and adults.

If a driver gets a distracted driving ticket for texting, the penalties are different from state to state. In California, for example, a driver would pay $20 for the first offense and $50 for additional offenses. In contrast, in Alaska, which has the toughest penalties, a distracted

Receiving tickets can add points to a driver's license and increase insurance rates. Enough points will result in the license being suspended.

driver can be charged with a misdemeanor, pay up to $10,000, and spend a year in prison.

Another consequence of distracted driving is adding points to a license. The point system is used by forty-one states to monitor a driver's driving record and determine whether or not his or her license should be suspended or revoked. Different driving infractions, such as speeding, running a red light, or texting while driving, are worth a certain number of points. In Georgia, a texting ticket adds one point to a driver's record. In New York, it adds five. Depending on the insurance company, getting points can also trigger an increase in insurance rates.

Drivers who rack up a certain number of points in a designated amount of time may lose their license. For example, in California, a driver's license will be suspended for six months and the driver will be on probation for a year if the driver gets four points in twelve months, six points in twenty-four months, or eight points in thirty-six months.

Legal Consequences of a Crash

If drivers are distracted and cause a minor crash, meaning there are no serious or permanent injuries, they may only receive a traffic ticket or add points on their license. But if a person is injured or killed in the crash, drivers can face criminal charges. Depending on state laws and the severity of the crash, the driver can be charged with a range of crimes and receive a range of consequences.

In Minnesota, a distracted driver who causes a minor crash can be charged with a misdemeanor, which has a maximum penalty of ninety days in prison and a $1,000 fine. In a more serious injury crash, the driver can be charged with a felony and receive up to five years in jail and a $10,000 fine. If the crash kills another person, the driver could receive felony charges such as vehicular manslaughter and receive up to ten years in jail and a $20,000 fine.

In Alaska, penalties are much harsher. A distracted driver who injures someone in a crash can be charged with a class C felony and receive a sentence of up to five years and a $50,000 fine. If a person is killed in the crash, the driver can be charged with a class A felony and receive up to twenty years in prison and a $250,000 fine.

Regardless of whether the distracted driver was charged or not, he can also be sued by the victim or the victim's family. If the victim is injured in the crash, she can file a personal injury lawsuit against the driver or his insurance company. This suit is to recover expenses that occurred as a result of the crash. Personal injury expenses include things like medical expenses, loss of income, property damage, and pain and suffering. If the victim dies in the crash, family members can file a wrongful death lawsuit to reclaim expenses from the driver or his or her insurance company. These expenses include hospitalization, loss of income and support, and funeral costs. Funeral costs alone can add up to thousands of dollars.

Usually, civil lawsuits do not go to trial. Instead, both parties reach an agreement, called a settlement. When a settlement is reached, the driver who caused the crash or his insurance company can be on the hook for tens of thousands or even hundreds of thousands of dollars. If the driver is under eighteen years old and is on his or her parents' insurance plan, the parents can also be held financially responsible. If the case does go to court, a jury determines whether money should be awarded to the victim, and if so, how much.

Crash Injuries

Though much attention is given to the number of people killed in distracted driving crashes each year, the number injured is much greater. In 2015, 391,000 people were injured in distracted driving crashes compared to 3,477 fatalities. Injuries can happen to the driver, passengers inside the car, people traveling in another vehicle, or cyclists and pedestrians. Sometimes these injuries are minor and the person can make a complete recovery. In other cases, the injuries are life altering, and the person will need ongoing care and support.

One common injury in a car crash is a traumatic brain injury. A minor traumatic brain injury, also called a concussion, can take from one to three months to heal. But a major traumatic brain injury can leave a person permanently disabled with complications such as delayed mental processing, loss of one or more senses, and lack of motor control.

Brad Gorski was twenty-one, driving the five-minute trip home from the gym, when he ran a red light while looking at his phone and was struck by a semi. Though the crash happened in 2005, Brad deals daily with the results of the traumatic brain injury he sustained, which slows his speech and motor skills. Despite these challenges, Brad speaks on the dangers of distracted driving. "I plead with everyone, put your phone down while driving," Gorski said in a TEDx talk.[46] "No text message is more important than your life."[47]

> **"I plead with everyone, put your phone down while driving. No text message is more important than your life."** [46]
>
> —Brad Gorski, car accident survivor

Injuries to the neck and spinal cord are also common in crashes. A minor injury, such as whiplash, may be corrected by a chiropractor or doctor. A more serious fracture or break in the neck or spine may require surgery. Neck injuries can also damage a person's spinal cord, the bundle of nerves that runs from the brain down through a person's spinal column. Severe damage to the spinal cord can lead to partial or full paralysis, altering a person's life forever.

In 2010, Xzavier Davis-Bilbo was paralyzed after being struck by a texting driver. Five-year-old Xzavier was crossing the street while holding his older sister's hand. They were nearly to the curb when a car ran a stop sign and struck Xzavier, dragging him down the street. If it wasn't for the metal scooter slung over his shoulder, Xzavier would likely have been killed. Instead, he was left paralyzed from the diaphragm down. He is now in a wheelchair and on a ventilator which must be monitored at all times.

A crash victim can also experience broken bones, damage to internal organs, and even the loss of limbs. Depending on the severity

Victims of severe car crashes can experience more than physical pain. Anxiety and PTSD can result from traumatic accidents.

of the damage, surgery may be required. And physical therapy may be necessary to regain mobility.

Aimee Eckert lost her leg in a distracted driving crash in 2011. Aimee was hit head-on by a woman going 75 miles per hour (121 km/h) in a 35-mile-per-hour (56 km/h) zone. The woman was texting. Doctors repaired Aimee's broken bones with plates and screws and repaired blood vessels in her heart. They were not able to save her left leg, however, which was amputated below the knee. But Aimee's greatest loss was that of her pregnancy. Aimee was six months pregnant at the time of the crash and her unborn baby, Gabriel, was killed.

Mental Health Consequences

Along with physical injuries, a crash victim can develop mental health problems. The victim may become depressed, especially if working to recover from serious physical challenges. The victim may experience anxiety around vehicles and driving, making it difficult for him or her to ride in a car again. The victim may also experience post-traumatic stress disorder (PTSD) and continue to have intense thoughts and feelings related to the crash afterward. Counseling and therapy may be needed to help a victim process these challenges in a healthy way.

Michael Vang, a Minnesota teen, killed former classmate David Riggs in a distracted driving crash in 2013. Though Michael didn't seek traditional counseling, his court-appointed community service with the Shreya R. Dixit Memorial Foundation served that role in his life.

"When I first met Michael, he could barely communicate. He was terrified, confused, shaken, and lost," said Vijay Dixit.[48] Over several months, Dixit took Michael to distracted driving events and counseled him to turn his tragedy into something positive. Through the process, Michael was able to open up about his experiences and even speak about them in front of a crowd.

"Coming out to walks, seeing new faces, and being a speaker made me strong, and that really helped me," Michael said of his experience.[49] Thanks to Dixit and his foundation, Michael was able to heal and give back to his community.

In addition, the mental health of the crash victim's family, friends, and coworkers can all be affected by the loss of someone they knew and loved. Children have to grow up without a parent. Families grieve the loss of a child. Sports teams say goodbye to a player. Companies lose a valuable employee. Every loss creates a circle of grief that spreads to each person the crash victim knew. Giana Mucci's mother, Sheryl, was killed by a distracted driver in 2015. Mucci describes her grief in an interview with *Cosmopolitan*:

> There are days when my anger toward this distracted driver consumes me. Days when saying "I love you, Mom" hurts. Some days, I'm okay. Sometimes, seeing a ladybug or dragonfly makes me smile. But most days, I just want to talk to my mom. That distracted driver didn't kill just one person that day in March. She killed me too.[50]

Witnesses to a distracted driving crash can also be affected, sometimes developing mental health problems due to the graphic images they witnessed. Like a crash victim, witnesses can experience depression, anxiety, and PTSD and may need professional counseling to recover.

> "Not looking for one minute can change entire families' lives."[54]
>
> —Kristin Talsma, mother of distracted driving victim

Ron Pumphrey, whose wife Michelle Begley was killed by a distracted driver, tells of a young man, Madison, who sought counseling after witnessing the crash. Madison and his friend were the first to approach Michelle's crumpled car, check for her pulse, and find she was no longer alive. As part of his grieving process, Madison reached out to Pumphrey. "I review [the crash] in slow motion every night before I go to sleep," Madison told him.[51] "That's an image that will never leave my head."[52]

Victims of Distracted Driving Crashes

Death is the most serious consequence of a distracted driving crash. Most often, the person killed is a driver. In 2015, 61 percent of distracted driving deaths were driver fatalities, either the distracted driver or another driver struck in the crash.

College student Alex Heit became a driver-fatality statistic in 2013 when he rolled his car in Greely, Colorado. The road he was navigating had a narrow shoulder and steep drop-off. According to witnesses, Alex had his head down and drifted into the oncoming lane. When he looked up, he jerked the wheel to the right, overcompensating, and his car rolled down the embankment. Alex's cell phone, which was recovered from the crash site, showed an incomplete text. Alex's last words were, "Sounds good my man, seeya soon, ill tw."[53]

In some distracted driving crashes, one or more passengers in the vehicle are killed. In 2015, 23 percent of those killed in distracted driving crashes were passengers, either in the car with the distracted driver or riding in a vehicle struck in the crash. David Talsma, age thirteen, was the passenger in the back seat of a minivan when he was killed by a distracted driver in 2015. The minivan, operated by his sixteen-year-old sister, was part of a pile-up on a freeway. The man who caused the crash confessed he was checking his GPS and eating a sandwich and didn't realize traffic on the highway was stopped due to construction. "Not looking for one minute can change entire families' lives," said David's mother, Kristin, in a local interview.[54]

In other crashes, someone outside the car dies. They may be a cyclist, pedestrian, or another person using the roadway. In 2015, 16 percent of people killed were outside a motor vehicle. Chandler Gerber was twenty-one in 2012 when the carpet cleaning van he was driving veered off the road, striking an Amish family's buggy and killing three children, ages three, five, and seventeen. Gerber was texting with his wife at the time. He now lives with the consequences of his choice. "I wish so bad I could go back to that day and change my focus," Gerber said in the documentary *From One Second to the Next*.[55] "I wish I could go back and say, 'ya know, I can

A family sued Snapchat over a driver using the speed filter while driving. The phone app would post the speed of the phone when a photo or video was taken.

do these texts when I get to my stop, when I get there, I don't have to do this now while I'm driving.' There's just nothing that important."[56]

People That Can Be Held Responsible

Though the driver is the one legally responsible for causing a crash, several civil court cases have tried to prove that other parties are also guilty of distracting the driver. None of these have been successful.

In 2012, David and Linda Kubert each lost a leg in a crash. They sued the eighteen-year-old driver, Kyle Best, and his girlfriend, Shannon Colonna, who had been texting with him. Though Colonna was not in the car, the Kuberts' lawyer argued she was "electronically present" at the time of the crash.[57] The appeals court judge found no evidence that Colonna knew Best was driving, but the judge's statement left the possibility open for future lawsuits. He said that if someone did know the person they were texting was driving, "it is not unfair to hold the sender responsible for the distraction."[58]

Two lawsuits have attempted to hold companies responsible for their role in distracted driving crashes. In 2015, Maynard Wentworth filed a lawsuit against Snapchat for the app's role in a distracted driving crash that left him with a debilitating brain injury. According to the lawsuit, the driver, Christal McGee, was using the app's feature which tracks a person's speed at the time of the photo. According to passengers, McGee photographed herself at 107 mph (172 km/h) and was posting the photo when she struck Wentworth's car.

The lawsuit blamed Snapchat for the crash. "Despite Snapchat's actual knowledge of the danger from using its product's speed filter while driving at excessive speeds, Snapchat did not remove or restrict access to the speed filter."[59] A judge dismissed the charges, saying Snapchat was immune from the complaint, citing the 1996 Communications Decency Act. Section 230 of this law states that companies that provide digital or online services cannot be held responsible for what their users do with the product.

Another lawsuit tried to hold Apple responsible for a distracted driving death. In 2016, a Texas family sued Apple because their five-year-old daughter was killed in a crash involving a driver who was using the company's video chat app, FaceTime. "The lawsuit claims the company failed 'to warn users that the product was likely to be dangerous when used or misused' or to instruct on its safe usage. It also cited a previous Apple patent and said the company failed to manufacture its iPhone 6 Plus with "safer, alternative 'lock-out' technology," reported the *International Business Times*.[60] The lawsuit was thrown out by a judge in May 2017. Apple did, however, add a "do not disturb while driving" feature to its 2017 iOS 11 operating system.

Chapter 4

HOW DRIVERS CAN PROTECT THEMSELVES AND GET HELP

It is clear that distracted driving can have serious consequences. But there are steps teen and adult drivers can take to protect themselves. From pledging to remain distraction-free to driving defensively, there are many ways a driver can prevent a crash.

Steps to Drive Distraction Free

First, teens and adults need to approach driving with a mindset of respect for everyone on the road. At the annual Raksha Walk, a safe-driving awareness event sponsored by the Shreya R. Dixit Memorial Foundation, participants receive a bracelet with a card that reads:

> *I PROMISE . . . To remember that everyone on the road is someone's sister, brother, mother, father, daughter, son or friend; to keep my eyes and mind on the road at all times—TO PROTECT YOU.*[61]

With this mindset, drivers aren't trying to see what they can get away with while driving. Instead, the driver is focused on keeping themselves and everyone else's loved ones safe.

Designating a passenger to navigate and use the phone instead of the driver is a safe alternative. This will allow the driver to keep his or her eyes on the road.

Along with a respectful mindset, teen drivers should follow these guidelines for driving distraction-free. First, limit the number of passengers in the car. Research shows the risk of a crash increases with each teen passenger, so teens should drive alone or with trusted friends as allowed by graduated license regulations in their state. Teens should also be careful about driving with pets or young children, as their needs can cause distractions.

Teens should also complete potentially distracting activities before driving or after the vehicle is safely stopped. They should adjust vehicle controls, such as the radio, mirrors, or climate controls, before starting to drive. In addition, they should pull over or wait until arriving at their destination to reach for an object behind the seat, look in the vanity mirror, put on makeup, drink a cup of coffee, eat a snack, take a phone call, or send a text.

Teens should also minimize distraction from electronics. Cell phones and other portable electronics should be kept out of sight. Instead of putting a phone in the cup holder or front console, it should be stored in the glove compartment or in a purse or backpack in the back seat or trunk. In addition, devices should be turned off or put on silent mode so that notification tones don't tempt a driver to check the screen. If using the navigation system in the car, drivers should type in the destination information before leaving and make sure the speaker is audible. If a driver does have to use the phone while driving, it is best to pull over to a safe location, stop, and then dial or type.

Planning for Safe Driving as a Family

Parents can set bad examples by using electronic devices while driving. In addition, parents expect their children to reply to calls and texts at all times. But, according to the End Distracted Driving (EndDD) website, families can work together to be part of the solution. "It's really not that difficult to know what to do to drive safer," says EndDD, "but sometimes it is difficult to change our driving behaviors, especially the use of portable electronic devices. Habits may be difficult to change unless we have a plan and commit to driving safer."[62]

EndDD suggests creating a family safe-driving agreement, a statement teens and parents sign to promise they will drive distraction-free. A sample plan, posted on the organization's website, encourages drivers to pledge "Yes! I will" to statements such as, "pull over to a safe location or wait until I am finished driving to eat or apply makeup," and, "when alone, turn my cell phone off before starting to drive."[63]

GAME OVER: CHILDREN CAN MAKE PARENTS BETTER DRIVERS

Creators of the PBS show *Ruff Ruffman Humble Media Genius* are enlisting children to help their parents and caretakers drive safely. PBS teamed up with media producer WGBH Boston and the Connecticut Department of Transportation to create Game Over, a distracted driving awareness campaign targeted at preschool- and elementary-aged children.

"Anecdotally, kids have been successful in encouraging their parents to quit smoking, to wear seatbelts and to recycle. When kids become vocal advocates, parents may change their habits," explains Bill Shribman, WGBH Senior Executive Producer and the project's creator.[1]

The team has created resources such as videos, games, and a safe-driving pledge for the PBS Kids website that teaches children the difference between safe and distracted driving. In one online video, the main character, Ruff Ruffman, sings the Driving Song. Its chorus is, "My name is Ruff and all I ask is when you drive, you don't multitask!"[2] The team hopes that kids can encourage the adults in their lives to drive safely and grow up to be better drivers themselves.

1. Quoted in "Connecticut Department of Transportation and WGBH Boston Launch Safe Driving Initiative with PBS Kids Character Ruff Ruffman," *WGBH Boston*, December 8, 2015. www.prnewswire.com.

2. "Ruff Ruffman Humble Media Genius: Driving," *PBS Kids*, 2017. pbskids.org.

Protection from Distracted Drivers

Even when a driver chooses to drive distraction-free, he or she may encounter unsafe drivers in other vehicles on the road. To avoid being hit by another car, a driver must practice defensive driving. "To drive defensively, we must anticipate that other drivers will make mistakes and will do the unexpected, often precipitating crashes. We need to be prepared for those mistakes to avoid crashes," says Joel Feldman, founder of EndDD.[64] Feldman uses the following example to explain how a defensive mindset can help a driver anticipate a crash:

As we approach an intersection, even if we have the green light, can we safely take our eyes off other cars expecting them to stop for their red traffic signal? Or, because of the prevalence of distracted driving, shouldn't we expect them to continue into the intersection against the red light because they are looking at their phones and not at the road?[65]

In addition to predicting a driver's bad behavior, driving experts give several other tips for defensive driving. First, drivers should look far ahead. New drivers tend to look directly in front of their car. Instead, drivers should look down the road as far as possible. This gives them the best perspective on what's happening around them and can help them better predict what other drivers will do.

It is also important for a driver to have an escape route. This means drivers should always have a place to move their vehicle, like the next lane or the road's shoulder, if their path is suddenly obstructed. To do this, drivers should position their car where they can both see the entire roadway and be seen by other drivers. They should also leave a safe space, called a buffer zone, between themselves

> **"It's really not that difficult to know what to do to drive safer, but sometimes it is difficult to change our driving behaviors, especially the use of portable electronic devices. Habits may be difficult to change unless we have a plan and commit to driving safer."[62]**
>
> —EndDD.org, *Be Part of the Solution: Together We Can End Distracted Driving*

and the cars around them, and should move out of the way if another vehicle is driving alongside them or following too closely.

In addition, drivers can maintain their buffer zone by keeping a safe following distance between themselves and the car ahead of them. The typical rule of thumb is to allow a minimum of two seconds between cars, but three is even better. At night, drivers should allow four seconds between cars. To gauge the distance between cars, drivers should count the number of seconds between when the car ahead passes a fixed object and when their car reaches it. With a safe following distance, drivers will have enough time to stop if the driver ahead slams on the brakes unexpectedly. If the roads are slippery, the following distance should be even greater, since rain, ice, or snow can make it harder to stop in time.

> **"Remember that as a passenger you are every bit as responsible for what goes on in a vehicle as the driver."[66]**
>
> —Hangupanddrive.com

Drivers interested in brushing up on their defensive driving skills can take a course either in person or online. Taking one will improve driving skills and may also qualify drivers for a reduction in their car insurance rate.

Keeping Drivers Undistracted

Safe-driving advocate Jacy Good encourages passengers to speak up for themselves if they are uncomfortable with the driver's behavior. "Remember that as a passenger you are every bit as responsible for what goes on in a vehicle as the driver." says Good's website, Hang Up and Drive.[66] Teen passengers, however, can often feel uncomfortable voicing their concern, especially if the driver is a parent or friend.

KidsHealth.org explains several ways passengers can encourage a driver to focus on the road. Though the tips are geared toward texting, they can apply to other distracting behaviors as well. Passengers should ask the driver directly to stop. If that doesn't work, the passenger can offer to be the designated texter and manage all communication, navigation, or music selecting duties. As a group, friends can take away the driver's keys, just as people do with drunk drivers. They can also avoid riding with a person who is known to practice distracted driving. If the driver doesn't listen, passengers should get out of the car as soon as it is safe and refuse to ride with that person in the future. Though teens may be nervous to confront a friend or parent, an AT&T End Distracted Driving Month survey showed that more than half (57 percent) "of drivers would stop using their phone if a friend asked them to."[67]

> "As a minimum, you need to train yourself to be considerate of everyone's safety when you are a passenger."[68]
>
> —EndDD.org

In addition to changing the driver's behavior, passengers must make sure they are not causing the distraction. "As a minimum, you need to train yourself to be considerate of everyone's safety when you are a passenger," the EndDD.org website says.[68] Passengers should refrain from singing loudly to music, throwing objects, arguing, or behaving in other ways that take the driver's attention off the road.

Organizations Promoting Distraction-Free Driving

Several companies and organizations are motivating drivers to drive distraction-free. Cell phone provider AT&T has created the It Can Wait campaign to inspire safe driving. One part of the campaign encourages drivers to post a photo of themselves on the website and agree to three key statements:

I pledge to care for those around me and put my phone down when driving.
I pledge to share the message: distracted driving is never okay.
I pledge to be aware that I'm never alone on the road.[69]

The It Can Wait website has collected over 23 million pledges. It Can Wait also airs television commercials that depict the dangers of distracted driving. One commercial, titled "No Post Is Worth a Life," shows slow-motion footage of a crash in reverse. Only at the end of the commercial does the viewer learn the crash was caused when a mother hears an alert tone, glances down at her phone, and tells her young daughter in the back seat, "Everyone likes the picture I posted of you."[70]

There are other organizations dedicated to educating students and the general public about the dangers of distracted driving as well. Many of these groups were founded by people who lost a loved one in a distracted driving crash. The Casey Feldman Memorial Foundation was started by Joel Feldman after his daughter Casey was killed in 2009. In addition to hosting the website EndDD, Feldman has given more than 400 presentations at schools and workplaces, is frequently quoted in the national media, and is a regular speaker at youth safety conferences.

It's not just adults who are speaking out against distracted driving. In 2011 Peter, Aaron, and Willa Berry lost their parents on a family road trip when their minivan was struck by a driver reaching in the back seat to change a movie for his daughter. As a result of the crash, Peter and Aaron both suffer from paraplegia. In 2014, the teens and their cousins started a campaign they call OLIE, which stands for One Life Is Enough. Willa described an OLIE event at their school in a 2016 video. "We're having a bake sale, but it's not really a bake sale. We're giving away free desserts to people who sign the pledge, and with that they'll get an OLIE bracelet," Willa said.[71] Like other safe-driving pledges, the OLIE pledge asks people to promise they will not engage in distracting activities while they drive. Thanks to a $10,000 grant from Allstate Insurance, the Berrys have been able to bring the OLIE program to other schools as well.

Technology That Can Help

If willpower and safe-driving pledges aren't enough, drivers can use apps to limit their cell phone's capabilities while a car is in motion. Some apps, like AT&T's DriveMode and the LifeSaver app, block calls, texts, and status updates. Other apps turn safe driving into a game. TrueMotion Family scores each driving trip, and family members can compare their scores to see who is the safest driver. Mojo tracks how often drivers interact with their phones and gives points for each minute they go without calling, typing, or swiping. Points can be used to earn gift cards and to compete with friends.

Though safe-driving apps can help drivers break bad habits and give parents peace of mind, they do have their limitations. One common complaint about safe-driving apps is that they must be turned on each time the driver gets behind the wheel. Another is they drain the phone's battery because they must remain running in the background. Some parents complain because motivated teens can find a way to circumvent the apps' restrictions and still use their phones while driving.

Because apps have limitations, companies have also developed devices that can be installed in a car to block cell phone use. Scott Tibbitts of Boulder, Colorado, has developed Groove, a rectangular black box which is plugged in under the steering wheel. Groove alerts the cell phone company to hold calls and texts, and it blocks the

Some car makers are adding safety features that can help brake. These sensors look for objects such as pedestrians in the road.

driver from making calls or sending messages. "Just when you start driving, you go into super airplane mode where the things that would distract you go away," Tibbits said in an interview with CNN.[72]

DriveID by Cellcontrol is a similar device that mounts on the windshield right behind the rearview mirror. DriveID starts when it senses the car is in motion and disables call, text, and social media functions on the driver's phone. It can be set to block the use of passengers' phones as well. DriveID is used by teens and families. It is also useful to companies who want to control employee phone use in company vehicles.

Though these hardware solutions do a better job of blocking cell use than apps, each device must be purchased. Also, Cellcontrol

THE ROAD TO ZERO FATALITIES

In October 2016, the NSC launched the Road to Zero Coalition. This group of public and private organizations is teaming up to reduce traffic fatalities to zero by 2050. As of November 2017, 460 organizations have joined the NSA in their quest. This list includes auto manufacturers, cities, universities, advocacy groups, and government agencies.

"A goal like this has been called a moon shot, and it may seem impossible. It's not impossible. It just hasn't been done yet," said Debbie Hersman of the NSC.[1] She notes that years go by without a single airline death. She believes the same is possible for roads.

To reach their goal, the coalition is working to raise public awareness about traffic fatalities. It has also given away $1 million in grants to groups working to end roadway deaths.

The city of Chicago plans to use its $185,000 grant to improve safety in neighborhoods on the city's west side. "We still experience far too many traffic crashes," mayor Rahm Emanuel said to the *Chicago Tribune*. "The status quo is unacceptable."[2]

1. National Safety Council, "Road to Zero Marks First Anniversary," *YouTube*, October 27, 2017. www.youtube.com.

2. Quoted in Mary Wisniewski, "City Releases Vision Zero Plan Aimed at Preventing Roadway Deaths, Injuries," *Chicago Tribune*, June 12, 2017. www.chicagotribune.com.

charges a monthly subscription fee. In contrast, many safe-driving apps are free.

Car Manufacturer Safety Steps

The auto industry has made many advancements in safety over the years. All cars are required to have safety features, such as seatbelts and airbags, to protect drivers and passengers in the event of a crash. Automakers also design cars with crumple zones. These areas of the vehicle are made to crush on impact, so they can absorb the energy of the crash.

The next generation of safety features, called Advanced Driver Assistance Systems (ADAS), do more than just protect drivers. They help drivers avoid a crash. Many of the features come standard on new cars, while others are still only found in luxury vehicles. But as the technology advances and becomes less expensive, it will continue to become more accessible to everyone.

Some ADAS features help prevent distracted driving crashes. For example, distracted drivers are prone to rear-end collisions because they don't realize the vehicle in front of them has slowed or stopped. To prevent this problem, the forward collision warning (FCW) system alerts drivers with an audible signal if they are approaching a car too quickly, giving drivers time to stop. When the driver applies the brakes suddenly, the assisted braking will electronically boost the car's braking power, helping the car stop as quickly as possible. If the sensors detect that a collision is imminent and the driver is not reacting, an automatic emergency braking (AEB) system will apply the brakes.

Most AEB systems start working when the car is traveling at higher speeds. For example, Subaru's Pre-Collision Braking System is activated when the car is traveling 30 mph (50 km/h) or higher. Some manufactures have developed AEB systems that work at in-town speeds, like Chevrolet's Low-Speed Forward Automatic Braking which activates at speeds of 5 to 37 mph (8 to 60 km/h). Some systems, like Volvo's Pedestrian Detection, can even detect and brake for people and cyclists, though these systems may not always work in low light or limited visibility situations. In a partnership with the NHTSA, twenty car companies have pledged to make AEB systems standard on all new cars by 2022.

Self-driving cars are not yet fully autonomous. Hands-free automobiles exist, but some form of driver engagement is still required.

Distracted drivers can also cause lane-departure crashes because they aren't aware when their vehicle is moving out of its lane. When a driver's car drifts slowly to the side, it can strike a vehicle or object next to him. A driver who suddenly realizes her car is drifting may turn hard to correct her steering and veer into oncoming traffic or off the road. To prevent this problem, a lane departure warning system tracks the lines on the highway and warns drivers with a visual or audio signal that their car has drifted out of the lane. Lane keeping assist systems can even take over steering and gently guide the car back into the lane.

Some new cars also come with alertness monitoring systems. These systems warn drivers if they are behaving in a way that's unsafe. For example, Cadillac's Super Cruise system monitors the driver with a camera in the steering wheel and ensures the driver's eyes remain on the road. According to an article in *Forbes*, "Should the driver be caught, say, reading a book or is applying makeup while in Super Cruise mode, the system will give a series of audible and visual warnings to tell him or her to refocus on the task at hand; if after continued warnings the system determines the motorist is unresponsive, it will bring the vehicle to a controlled stop and, if necessary, contact first responders."[73]

Some warn, however, that these ADAS features may actually increase distracted driving crashes in the short-term. They may well lull a driver into a false sense of security. As a result, the driver may continue his or her distracted behavior behind the wheel, making it hard for the driver to reengage when he or she is needed to step in and control the vehicle.

Self-Driving Cars

In the future, drivers may not even be necessary. Self-driving, or autonomous, vehicles would remove the possibility for human error and avoid most if not all crashes seen today. These cars are currently in the works, with companies like Uber and Google racing to develop the necessary technology.

Currently, Tesla's Autopilot and Cadillac's Super Cruise mode allow the driver to take his or her foot off the brakes and hands off the wheel while driving on the highway. But these cars are not fully autonomous and require the driver to pilot the car on neighborhood streets and in bad weather conditions.

However, *Fortune* magazine predicts that by 2040, 95 percent of cars on the road will be self-driving. And this could mean the end of distracted driving and other road fatalities because the number one cause of crashes, human error, is eliminated. An article by Adrienne Roberts in the *Wall Street Journal* describes the self-driving car future this way:

> There will be no need for traffic lights because the vehicles will be able to communicate with each other to time when they go through the intersection. The cars will intuitively know what's a safe speed to travel based on traffic and road conditions. And human errors such as failing to stop at a stop sign or mistakenly driving through a red light will become nonissues.[74]

Though a future with self-driving cars appears rosy, some warn it may not arrive as quickly or be as beneficial as predicted. One factor that may slow the adoption of self-driving cars is public perception. A 2017 AAA Foundation survey found that three-quarters of Americans were afraid of riding in self-driving cars and only one in ten felt self-driving cars would make the roads safer. Reasons for this apprehension include fears the technology will fail, fears the operating system could be hacked, and fears that personal information stored in the car's computer could be stolen.

Another factor that could slow the roll-out of autonomous vehicles is the condition of America's roads. For self-driving cars to navigate safely, lane lines on roads need to be painted clearly and intersections need to be outfitted with systems that relay data to cars. Some experts, like Tennessee DOT Commissioner John Schroer, compare the change needed to the one that took place over one hundred years ago when Americans transitioned from horses to cars. Though some states, like California and Michigan, are beginning to make changes, there is not yet a nation-wide plan to upgrade roads.

Whether or not self-driving cars can end traffic fatalities in the future, it is clear, that driving in the United States today is dangerous for everyone. There are nearly 6.4 million traffic crashes and 40,000 traffic fatalities annually. And driving is most dangerous for teens, who experience more crashes and fatalities than any other age group. Since most crashes are caused by human error, roads won't get safer unless drivers change their behaviors. Choosing to drive distraction-free could save thousands of lives each year.

Though cell phone use, especially texting, is synonymous with distracted driving, there are many other activities, like eating or reaching for an object, that can take a driver's attention from the road. When this happens, the consequences can be both expensive and life-changing for the driver and other crash victims. Fortunately, many people are working hard to end distracted driving. Researchers, lawmakers, and safe-driving advocates are working together to pass stricter regulations and to educate the public about the dangers of their behaviors. Auto manufactures are working to create new technology to make current cars safer. But in the end, the change is in the hands of the teen or adult behind the wheel. America's roads will only be safer when its drivers choose to drive distraction-free.

> **"And human errors such as failing to stop at a stop sign or mistakenly driving through a red light will become nonissues."[74]**
>
> —Adrienne Roberts, *Wall Street Journal*

RECOGNIZING SIGNS OF TROUBLE

How often do you do each of these activities while you drive?

- Change channels on the radio
- Put on makeup
- Check appearance in vanity mirror
- Reach for an object
- Talk on a handheld cell phone
- Look at GPS map or directions
- Take a photo
- Sing along exuberantly with a song
- Have a conversation with a teen passenger
- Drive with young children or pets in the vehicle

Ways to Avoid Distracted Driving

- Place cell phone in an inaccessible place while driving
- Turn the phone off or put it in safe-driving mode
- Pull over or park in a safe location to make important phone calls or send text messages
- Designate a passenger to manage navigation, music selection, and cell phone communications
- Enter address into GPS and preview the route before leaving for the destination
- Secure all objects and food being transported
- Eat, drink, and take care of personal grooming before leaving or after arriving
- Follow local distracted driving and novice driver laws

ORGANIZATIONS TO CONTACT

End Distracted Driving (Casey Feldman Foundation)

www.enddd.org

Joel Feldman founded this organization after his daughter was killed by a distracted driver. The website is a project of the foundation and provides distracted driving resources from across the internet.

Hang Up and Drive (Jacy and Steve Good)

www.hangupanddrive.com

Founded by distracted driving victim Jacy Good and her husband Steve, Hang Up and Drive promotes safe driving for students and adults.

National Highway Traffic Safety Administration (NHTSA)

www.nhtsa.gov

The NHTSA conducts crash tests and investigates vehicle defects. The agency collects national traffic data and provides safety education to the public.

National Safety Council's Survivor Advocate Network

www.nsc.org/act/Pages/nsc-survivor-advocate-network.aspx

The NSC provides support to crash victims and their families through the Survivor Advocate Network. The network helps people affected by a crash to share their stories and connect with other survivors. It also supports victims when they speak with the media and policy makers to encourage future change.

SOURCE NOTES

Introduction: A Napkin Can Turn a Father into an Activist

1. Quoted in Dan Hanzun, "Nate Burleson Posts Photos of Pizza Caused Car Wreck," *NFL,* October 1, 2013. www.nfl.com.

2. USDOTNHTSA, "Liz Mark's Texting and Driving Story," *YouTube,* April 25, 2014. www.youtube.com.

3. Vijay Dixit, *One Split Second: The Distracted Driving Epidemic. How It Kills and How We Can Fix It.* Somerville, MA: Wisdom Publications, 2016. pp. 32–33.

4. Vijay Dixit, *One Split Second: The Distracted Driving Epidemic. How It Kills and How We Can Fix It,* p. 43.

5. Quoted in "Eden Prairie's Vijay Dixit Wants to End Distracted Driving," *Southwest Metro Magazine,* October 2016. www.southwestmetromag.com.

6. Neal E. Boudette, "Biggest Spike in Traffic Deaths in 50 Years? Blame the Apps," *New York Times*, November 15, 2016. www.nytimes.com.

Chapter 1: What Is Distracted Driving?

7. "Distracted Driving 2015," *National Highway and Traffic Safety Administration*, March 2017. crashstats.nhtsa.dot.gov.

8. Ray LaHood, "For Better or Worse, Webster's 2009 Word of the Year: Distracted Driving," *The White House: President Barack Obama*. January 10, 2010. obamawhitehouse.archives.gov.

9. Noah Budnick, "Largest Distracted Driving Behavior Study," *Zendrive*, April 2017. blog.zendrive.com.

10. "Largest Distracted Driving Behavior Study."

11. Cher Carney, Dan McGehee, Karisa Harland, Madonna Weiss, and Mireille Raby, "Using Naturalistic Driving Data to Examine Teen Driving Behaviors Present in Motor Vehicle Crashes 2007–2015," *AAA Foundation for Traffic Safety*, June 2016. www.aaafoundation.org.

12. Quoted in Kyle Stock, "Distracted Driving Is More Deadly Than Data Shows: Special Report," *Insurance Journal,* October 18, 2017. www.insurancejournal.com.

13. Quoted in "Distracted Driving Is More Deadly Than Data Shows: Special Report."

14. Neal Lerner, Carryl Baldwin, James Stephen Higgins, and Jonathan Schooler, "Mind Wandering While Driving: What Does it Mean and What Do We Do About It?" *Proceedings of the Human Factors and Ergonomics Society Annual Meeting*, September 25, 2015. pp. 1686–1690.

15. Quoted in Tamara Johnson, "Young Millenials Top List of Worst Behaved Drivers," *AAA Newsroom*, February 15, 2017. newsroom.aaa.com.

16. Quoted in "Young Millennials Top List of Worst Behaved Drivers."

17. Quoted in "Employer Ban Cell Phone Policy Case Study," *National Safety Council*, 2015. www.nsc.org.

18. Quoted in "Employer Ban Cell Phone Policy Case Study,"

19. Anne T. McCartt, Kidd, David G. Teoh, Eric R., "Driver Cellphone and Texting Bans in the United States: Evidence of Effectiveness," *EndDD.org,* March 31, 2014. www.enddd.org.

20. "Largest Distracted Driving Behavior Study."

21. Quoted in Carol Cruzan Morton, "Why Cell Phone Bans Don't Work," *Science*, August 22, 2012. www.sciencemag.org.

Chapter 2: The Causes of Distracted Driving

22. Quoted in Sebastian Murdock, "Our Addiction to Cell Phones Is Costing Lives. Here's How We Can Stop It," *Huffington Post*, June 9, 2015. www.huffingtonpost.com.

23. Quoted in "Our Addiction to Cell Phones Is Costing Lives. Here's How We Can Stop It."

24. Quoted in "Our Addiction to Cell Phones Is Costing Lives. Here's How We Can Stop It."

25. Quoted in "Our Addiction to Cell Phones Is Costing Lives. Here's How We Can Stop It."

26. Quoted in Michael Dahr, "Is the Teen Brain More Vulnerable to Addiction?" *Huffington Post*, January 25, 2014. www.huffingtonpost.com.

27. Quoted in "Is the Teen Brain More Vulnerable to Addiction?"

28. Quoted in Anderson Cooper, "What Is "Brain Hacking"? Tech Insiders on Why You Should Care," *CBS*, April 9, 2017. www.cbsnews.com.

29. TEDPartners. "The Distracted Mind," *YouTube*, December 16, 2013.

30. Michael Aguilar and Megan N. Shoji, "Influencing Behavioral Intentions Toward Texting and Driving: Lessons Learned from a Multifaceted Prevention Campaign," *Innocorp, Ltd*, 2013. www.icadtsinternational.com.

31. "Roundtable: Act to End Deadly Distractions," *National Transportation Safety Board*, April 26, 2017. www.ntsb.gov.

32. Quoted in Vijay Dixit, *One Split Second: The Distracted Driving Epidemic. How It Kills and How We Can Fix It*, p. 92.

33. Quoted in Vijay Dixit, *One Split Second: The Distracted Driving Epidemic. How It Kills and How We Can Fix It*, p. 100.

34. Quoted in Lily Puckett, "Your 'Responsible Friend' May Actually Be More Likely to Engage in This Risky Behavior," *Teen Vogue*, April 18, 2016. teenvogue.com.

35. Quoted in Katherine Shonesy, "Personality May Dictate How Distracted You Are While Driving," *Science Daily*, April 12, 2016. www.sciencedaily.com.

36. Quoted in Stefan Kiesbye, *Distracted Driving.* Detroit, MI: Greenhaven Press, 2012. p. 15.

37. Noelle LaVoie, "Parents Part of the Problem in Distracted Teen Driving, Study Finds," *American Psychological Association*, August 7, 2014. www.apa.org.

38. LaVoie, "Parents Part of the Problem in Distracted Teen Driving, Study Finds."

39. "Parents Part of the Problem in Distracted Teen Driving, Study Finds."

40. Susan Yum, "Cell Phones and Driving Is the New Drunk Driving," *Huffington Post*, January 26, 2014. www.huffingtonpost.com.

41. Quoted in gocognitive, "David Strayer—Driver Distraction and Cell Phones," *YouTube*, November 3, 2011. www.youtube.com

42. Quoted in Fredrick Kunkle, "How to Reduce Distracted Driving in the Same Way as Drunk Driving? Shame," *The Chicago Tribune*, May 1, 2017. www.chicagotribune.com.

43. Quoted in "How to Reduce Distracted Driving in the Same Way as Drunk Driving? Shame."

44. Quoted in "How to Reduce Distracted Driving in the Same Way as Drunk Driving? Shame."

Chapter 3: Costs and Risks of Distracted Driving

45. "Car Insurance for Teen After Accident," *AutoInsurance*, n.d. www.autoinsurance.org.

46. TEDx Talks. "The Risks of Distracted Driving: Brad Gorski: TEDxStanley Park," *YouTube*, June 19, 2015. www.youtube.com.

47. "The Risks of Distracted Driving: Brad Gorski: TEDxStanley Park."

48. Vijay Dixit. *One Split Second: The Distracted Driving Epidemic. How It Kills and How We Can Fix It*, p. 49.

49. Vijay Dixit. *One Split Second: The Distracted Driving Epidemic. How It Kills and How We Can Fix It*, p. 175.

50. Quoted in Jennifer Chen, "My Mother's Killer Was Fined $250," *Cosmopolitan*, September 9, 2016. cosmopolitan.com.

51. Ron Pumphrey, Personal Interview, November 9, 2017.

52. Ron Pumphrey, Personal Interview, November 9, 2017.

53. "Alex Heit, 22 – CO." *enddd.org*, n.d. enddd.org.

54. Quoted in Alex Shabad, "Parents of Teen Killed Share Message on Distracted Driving," *WZZM*, August 5, 2015. www.wzzm13.com.

55. "From One Second to the Next," *YouTube*, August 7, 2013. www.youtube.com.

56. "From One Second to the Next."

57. Mark Strassmann, "Suing the Sender: Distracted Driving Lawsuit Blames Both Texters for Crash," *CBS News*, May 23, 2012. www.cbsnews.com.

58. Ben Seal, "Texting a Distracted Driver Could Now Bring Liability," *The Legal Intelligencer*, April 29, 2016. www.law.com.

59. Mary Beth Quirk, "Lawsuit Accuses Snapchat of Negligence for Speed Capturing Filter," *Consumerist*, April 28, 2016. consumerist.com.

60. Denisse Moreno, "Judge Throws Out Lawsuit that Blamed Apple for Distracted Driving," *International Business Times*, August 26, 2017.

Chapter 4: How Drivers can Protect Themselves and Get Help

61. "Sign Our Pledge to Drive Distraction Free," *shreyadixit.org*, n.d. shreyadixit.org.

62. "Be Part of the Solution: Together We Can End Distracted Driving," *EndDD.org*, n.d. www.enddd.org.

63. "Family Safe Driving Agreement," *EndDD.org*, n.d. www.enddd.org.

64. Joel Feldman, "Rethinking Defensive Driving in Light of Distracted Driving," *EndDD.org*, April 17, 2017. www.enddd.org.

65. "Rethinking Defensive Driving in Light of Distracted Driving."

66. "Hang Up and Drive," *Hang Up And Drive*, n.d. www.hangupanddrive.com.

67. Carmen Gonzalez Caldwell, "Say 'Yes' to the Prom but 'No' to Distracted Driving," *Miami Herald*, May 10, 2017. www.miamiherald.com.

68. "End Distracted Driving: When You're the Passenger," *EndDD.org,* October 5, 2011. www.enddd.org.

69. "Take the Pledge to Never Drive Distracted," *www.itcanwait.com*, n.d. www.itcanwait.com.

70. Cause Marketing, "AT&T 'It Can Wait' Campaign—TV Ad: 'No Post is Worth a Life,'" *YouTube*, June 19, 2016. www.youtube.com.

71. "Olie," *StopDistractions.org*, 2016. www.stopdistractions.org.

72. Quoted in Kelly Wallace, "Distracted Driving: Urging Companies to Crack Down," *CNN*, April 4, 2017. www.cnn.com.

73. Jim Gorzelany, "Ten Breakthrough New-Car Features for 2018," *Forbes*, August 25, 2017. www.forbes.com.

74. Adrienne Roberts, "Can Auto Fatalities Go to Zero?" *Wall Street Journal*, June 23, 2017. www.wsj.com.

FOR FURTHER RESEARCH

BOOKS

Vijay Dixit, *One Split Second: The Distracted Driving Epidemic: How It Kills and How We Can Fix It*. Somerville, MA: Wisdom Editions, 2016.

Stefan Kiesbye, editor, *Distracted Driving*. Farmington Hills, MI: Greenhaven Press, 2012.

Carla Mooney, *Thinking Critically: Cell Phones*. San Diego, CA: ReferencePoint, 2014.

Matt Richtel, *A Deadly Wandering*. New York: HarperCollins, 2014.

Gail B. Stewart, *Cell Phones and Distracted Driving*. San Diego, CA: ReferencePoint, 2015.

INTERNET SOURCES

Cher Carney, Dan McGehee, Karisa Harland, Madonna Weiss, and Mireille Raby, "Using Naturalistic Driving Data to Examine Teen Driving Behaviors Present in Motor Vehicle Crashes 2007-2015," *AAA Foundation for Traffic Safety*, June 2016. aaafoundation.org.

"Distracted Driving 2015," *National Highway and Traffic Safety Administration*, March 2017. crashstats.nhtsa.dot.gov.

"Traffic Safety Fact: Young Drivers," *National Highway and Traffic Safety Administration*, February 2017. nhtsa.gov.

"Understanding the Distracted Brain," *National Safety Council*, April 2012. www.nsc.org.

AT&T, "From One Second to the Next," *YouTube*, August 7, 2013. www.youtube.com.

TEDPartners, "The Distracted Mind," *YouTube*, December 16, 2013. www.youtube.com.

U.S. Department of Transportation, "Faces of Distracted Driving," *YouTube*, n.d. www.youtube.com.

WEBSITES

AAA Foundation for Traffic Safety

www.aaafoundation.org

This site contains reports of the organization's traffic safety studies, including several on distracted driving.

End Distracted Driving

www.enddd.org

Started by Joel Feldman, this site contains information and research on the dangers of distracted driving and how to prevent it.

It Can Wait (AT&T)

www.itcanwait.com/social

A safe-driving campaign by AT&T teaches about distracted driving and encourages drivers to pledge to drive distraction-free.

NHTSA Distracted Driving

www.distraction.gov

This government site contains facts and research reports.

INDEX

AAA Foundation for Traffic Safety, 15, 16–19, 66

Advanced Driver Assistance Systems, 63–65

Alaska, 41, 43

American Automobile Association, 7

Apple, 51

apps, 9, 10, 28, 51, 60, 62

AT&T, 25, 58, 59, 60

automatic emergency braking system, 63

Bailey, Stephen, 17

Begley, Michelle, 13, 48

Berry, Willa, 59–60

Best, Kyle, 50–51

Blakemore, Sarah-Jayne, 32

brain development, 24, 27, 32

brain injuries, 44–45, 51

Budnick, Noah, 14

Burleson, Nate, 4

Cadillac, 65

California, 40, 41, 43, 66

Casey Feldman Memorial Foundation, 59

cell phone addiction, 26–29

Chevrolet, 63

Chicago, Illinois, 37, 62

children, 11, 36, 47, 49, 53, 54, 55

Common Sense Media, 25, 27

Cummins, 21

cyclists, 14, 18, 44, 49, 63

Davis-Bilbo, Xzavier, 45

Dayton, Mark, 6

defensive driving, 52, 55–57

distracted driving laws, 12, 19–21, 22–23, 26, 40–44

Distraction-Free Driving clubs, 7

Dixit, Vijay, 5, 7, 8–9, 47

DriveID, 61

driver's license points, 42–43

driving distractions
  avoiding, 52–54
  cell phone use, 10–16, 19, 21, 23, 24–29, 54
  eating, 4, 11, 17, 20–21, 49, 67
  mental distractions, 11, 23, 30

drunk driving, 11, 15, 16, 22, 36–37, 58

Eckert, Aimee, 46
Emanuel, Rahm, 62
End Distracted Driving, 54

fatalities, 7, 8–9, 14–15, 18–19, 39, 44, 49, 62, 65–67
Feldman, Joel, 56, 59
felonies, 43
Fielkow, Brian, 32
financial costs, 38–39
forward collision warning system, 63
From One Second to the Next, 49

Georgia, 42
Gerber, Chandler, 49
Good, Jacy, 57
Google, 28, 65
Gorski, Brad, 45
Graduated Driver's Licensing, 21
Greenfield, David, 27

Hagerty, McKeel, 17
hands-free laws, 12, 21, 23, 26
Harris, Tristan, 28
Heit, Alex, 48, 49
Hersman, Debbie, 62
Hyneman, Jamie, 26

inattention blindness, 31
injuries, 14, 18, 38, 39, 43, 44–46, 51
insurance, 9, 17, 38, 39–40, 42, 43–44, 57
Insurance Institute for Highway Safety, 22
It Can Wait, 58–59

Kubert, David, 50
Kubert, Linda, 50

LaHood, Ray, 12
LaVoie, Noelle, 35–36
legal consequences, 19–23, 40–44
Liberty Mutual Insurance, 35
Los Angeles, California, 23

Marks, Liz, 5
mental health, 47–48
Michigan, 30, 66
Minnesota, 5, 6, 7, 34, 43, 47
misdemeanors, 42, 43
Missouri, 41
Morris, Nichole, 34
Mucci, Giana, 48
multitasking, 17, 29–31, 55
Mythbusters, 26

National Highway Transportation Safety Administration, 5, 10, 14, 16, 38–39, 63
National Institutes of Health, 35
National Safety Council, 16, 21, 26, 31, 35, 62
New York, 12, 42

Obama, Barack, 21
One Life Is Enough, 59–60
optimism bias, 31
Ouimet, Marie Claude, 33

pedestrians, 14, 18, 30, 44, 49, 63
Pew Research Center, 13, 35
Pokémon Go, 10
police, 12, 18, 21, 23, 40–41
post-traumatic stress disorder, 47, 48
Pumphrey, Ron, 48

Reimer, Bryan, 23
Riggs, David, 47
Road to Zero Coalition, The, 62

safe driving guidelines, 52–54
Savage, Adam, 26
Schroer, John, 66
seatbelts, 15, 18, 33, 34, 55, 62
self-driving cars, 65–67
Shreya R. Dixit Memorial Foundation,
    5–7, 47, 52
Shribman, Bill, 55
Siegel, Daniel, 27
Smith, Jennifer, 15
Snapchat, 28, 51
SPIDER method, 30
State Farm, 25
state laws, 19–21, 22–23, 26, 41–43
Stavrinos, Despina, 34
Strayer, David, 30, 37
Students Against Destructive
    Decisions, 35
Subaru, 63

Talsma, David, 49
Tennessee, 66
Tesla, 65
Texas, 12, 51
Tibbitts, Scott, 60

Uber, 65

Wentworth, Maynard, 51
Wiernimont, Clint, 21
Winstin, Jay A., 37

Vang, Michael, 47
Volvo, 63

Yang, David, 18, 19
Yum, Susan, 36–37

IMAGE CREDITS

ABOUT THE AUTHOR

Jennifer Simms is an educator and freelance writer in Boulder, Colorado. Her good friend and fellow writer Michelle Begley was killed by a distracted driver in 2015.